Tom Brady

The Incredible Story of Tom Brady – One of Football's Greatest Players!

Table of Contents

Introduction

Thank you and congratulations for taking the time to read this book!

This book serves as a biography to date of Tom Brady, the NFL superstar. In the following pages, you will learn just why Tom Brady is considered to be a legend of the game.

You will soon learn about Tom Brady's younger years, and how he was molded in to one of the best players the NFL has ever seen. You will also discover his greatest career moments, and what kind of performances and records he will be most remembered for.

This book also takes a look at Brady's life outside of football, and what might be next for the superstar.

Once again, thanks for choosing this book. I hope you find it to be both informative and enjoyable!

Chapter One: Early Life

Thomas Edward Patrick Brady Jr., popularly known as Tom Brady for short was born on the 3rd of August in the year 1977 in San Mateo in California. Tom is the fourth child of Thomas Brady Sr. And Galynn Patricia. Tom's father's ancestors were Irish while his mother Patricia had ties with Norway, Poland, and Sweden. Tom is the youngest and only boy child of his family, born after his three elder sisters named Nancy, Julie and Maureen. As a child, Tom was raised in a Catholic environment.

Tom started idolizing Joe Montana who was a quarterback of San Francisco 49ers when he regularly started attending the football games held at Candlestick Park in the 1980s. Tom was only four when the 1981 NFC championship took place. This was the championship in which the San Francisco 49ers beat the Dallas cowboys with "The catch", popularly known as such because of the winning touch down thrown by Joe Montana and caught by Dwight Clark. Joe Montana readily became Tom's inspiration. Tom was taught how to throw a football at a football camp organized at College of San Mateo by the camp counselor Tony Graziani who himself became an NFL/AFL quarterback in the coming future.

Brady's schooling took place in Junípero Serra High School where he started playing in the football and baseball teams of the school. Brady graduated from High school in 1995 and the graduation ceremony was organized at St. Mary's cathedral. He even got the chance to play against Pat Burrell who played Baseball and Football for Bellarmine College preparatory. Tom Brady began his Football journey with Padres JV team where he was initially just a backup quarter. The team wasn't fairing well that particular year with no touchdowns the whole year. Brady's luck changed when the starting quarterback suffered an injury and he was allowed to play in his place. Tom Brady ascended to become the varsity starter in his junior year right up until his graduation. In his senior year, Brady went to a lot of effort to get college coaches to notice him. Tom sent highlight tapes to the schools he was interested in joining which worked in his favor to put him on the radar of several football programs residing across the nation.

Around that time, the recruitment process was not like the current times and the ranking of the athletes was not as considerable as now, if it were, Brady would crash a four-star rating as a quarterback. Tom Brady had managed to make it to Blue Chip Illustrated and a Prep Football report All-American selection. Brady's father shared that Brady shortlisted his preference list to only five of the schools which were Cal-Berkeley, UCLA, USC, Michigan, and Illinois. Brady also had a good chance in baseball with his remarkable skills as a powerful hitting catcher. He was known for his exceptional baseball play in High school. The Montreal Expos even drafted him in the 18th round of 1995 MLB Draft when his field performance caught the attention of some MLB scouts. However, between Baseball and Football, Brady chose to pursue football as his ultimate passion.

Tom's ultimate choice turned out to be the university of Michigan when he was appointed by Bill Harris, Michigan Assistant and hence, Tom started playing for them in 1995. Tom's high school football career was as mesmerizing as one could expect, with 31 touchdowns and a record of 236 passes completed out of 447 for 3,702 yards under his name, Brady bagged many sorts of achievements out of which All-Far and All-state Honours and the most valuable player of the team award were most highlighting. Tom Brady did an internship at Merrill Lynch in the summers of 1998 and 1999. Further into 2003, Tom Brady was honored greatly by the Junípero Serra High

School when they inducted him into their Hall of fame along with many of the other graduates and his own elder sibling Maureen. Not only that, during Brady's visit at the school after the Super Bowl XLVI, the school administrators were so proud they made the announcement that their football stadium would be recognized by the name of "Brady Family Stadium".

College Career

Tom Brady played football in college for four years from 1995 to 1999. Initially, Brady started off as a backup quarterback at the University of Michigan's football team and held this position for two years. Meanwhile, around the same time, Brian Griese who later became a teammate and quarterback to Brady in the NFL, brought victory to the 1997 Wolverines in that first season. This was followed by the win in the Rose Bowl and a share of the National Championship. Brady's football career in college was not a walk in the park by any means; the way to the success was laid with obstacles. Brady was ranked seventh on the depth card and didn't have much luck getting to play on the field. This frustration and anxiety took a toll on him to the point where he had to consult a sports psychiatrist. He was disheartened and contemplated moving over to California. Greg Harden who was the assistant athletic director around that time mentored Brady and helped him get his confidence back.

Tom Brady was against Drew Henson in the race to become the starting quarterback under the coaching of Lloyd Carr, the head coach of Michigan. Eventually, it was Brady who got the starting position and held that position for the entirety of two seasons in 1998 and 1999. Brady as a starter took the team to new heights, and its success could be signified by the new record of most attempted and completed passes in a season set by the Michigan team which added up to a total of 214. Brady's name starred in the All-Big Ten honorable mentions in those two seasons. He was also given the position of Team Captain in his senior year. With Tom Brady as the starting quarterback, his team 'The wolverines' bagged 20 victories out of a total of 25 matches, which was a remarkable achievement. Another record was made by the team in 1998, which was for the completions in a game they lost to the Ohio state with a score of 31-16. The season was won with a merry victory against Arkansas in the Citrus Bowl.

The season of 1999 was another year that Brady served as a starting quarterback for Michigan state. The starting job was shared between Brady and Henson over the first 7 games of the season in which Brady would start for the first quarter, passing the job to Henson for the second while starting quarterback for the second half of the game would be appointed by coach Carr. The season began with Wolverines winning with a low score of 5-0 in the first game; in this same season they also defeated Notre Dame with a 26-22 total, and ultimately beat Wisconsin also. When in a match against Michigan State Brady was not playing in the second half, the team was struggling on the field with a deficit of 17 points. It was then when Tom Brady returned to the field and under his starting, the team made a wonderful recovery. However, they still lost by a score of 34-31 but that game, as well as the 300-yard passing game, played just the next week were important contributing factors in Coach Carr's decision to let Brady start for the rest of the season. Brady's starting career in college was filled with his team making brilliant recoveries in the last quarters on multiple occasions, the most notable of them being the victory against Penn State with a score of 31-27 and another victory over Indiana with a 34-31 final score. This win qualified the team for the season's Finals. This earned Tom Brady the title of 'Comeback Kid'.

The game against Ohio State in the regular season was crucial for Michigan as it was a ticket to the Orange Bowl. The game was tense with both teams going against each other with a score of 17-17 with only five minutes to spare. Brady saved the game in the end by scoring against Ohio State and leading the team into The Orange Bowl where yet again, they stood victorious over Alabama. The game was won with Brady leading the Team back from back to back 14-point deficits in both halves with four touchdowns and 369 yards thrown. The final straw to winning the game was Brady's throw to Shawn Thompson, leading Michigan towards victory. The win was made easier with the loss of an extra point by Alabama as a result of their own touchdown.

During the seasons Brady played for Michigan as a starter, he made a few good records out of which the biggest two were the wins in the Orange Bowl and the Citrus Bowl. Brady's career in Michigan came to a close with remarkable statistics. He fell third on the ranking list in the history of Michigan with 710 attempted and 442 completed throws, fourth with 5,351 yards and a completion percentage of 62.3, and fifth for a total of 35 touchdown passes.

Chapter Two: Making the NFL

Brady was not taken for the brilliant player he was when he first got out of college. One would expect him to be snatched right out of college by some big football organization after his remarkable performance in his junior and senior years. Rather, it took until the 6th round of the 2000 NFL Draft for the New England Patriots to draft Tom Brady. After that, Brady stuck to the New England Patriots for the entirety of his football career.

Brady's football career is garnished with the various titles and achievements he earned with his hard work and zest for Football. Brady registered a total of five super bowl victories under his name and was elected as the most valuable player in four Super Bowls and two leagues. With such a great record, Brady has made a lasting impact on the history of the NFL as one of the greatest quarterbacks of all time.

Tom Brady's achievements do not end there however, his records include being a twelve times nominee to the Pro Bowl as well as some monikers following his success in the field of football. Brady brought the Patriots to new heights of success, under his position as a starting quarterback, the Patriots registered 14 division titles under their name. Brady has been the best of the quarterbacks, as no other holds as many post-season wins as him. In the AFC Championship games, the patriots participated in a total of 11 seasons during the time period of 2001 to 2016 and stood victor in seven of those.

The starting job became Tom Brady's in the second season when Drew Bledsoe who was originally the starting quarterback was met with an injury and had to be replaced. Ultimately it was under Tom Brady's starting performance that the Patriots took the top spot in 36th Super Bowl. In the coming season, the

Patriots could not make it in the playoffs but afterward, they again took the championship in 2003 and 2004. Despite the continued marvelous gameplay, Tom Brady and the Patriots came back to participate in the Super Bowl again in 2007. This season set new records for the Patriots as they won with a remarkable score of 16 to 0. It was in this same season that Brady was first honored with the title of League MVP and hit another record for the most touchdown passes.

After this great win, it was disappointing for the Patriots to lose their championship title against the New York Giants during the season of Super Bowl XLII. Brady suffered a knee injury in the very first game of the year and could not play for the rest of the season. However, it did not take long for Tom and the Patriots to make a wonderful recovery in the 2009 season where they again stood strong against their competitors and played spectacularly. Brady had another accolade added to his account in this season when he was honored with National Football League Comeback Player of the Year Award, while in the next season; he won his second league MVP achievement.

The patriots once again suffered an inauspicious fate in the 2011 season where the New York Giants overpowered them for a second time. After that, Brady played his sixth Super Bowl season in 2014. This season took a historical turn when under Brady's starting job, the Patriots made a terrific recovery in the final and fourth quarter of the match against the Seattle Seahawks. Judging by the first three-quarters of the game, the outcome was entirely unexpected when the defending champion Seahawks lost and the Patriots once again stood victor. It was the fourth time the Patriots had won the Super Bowl and the third time that Brady won the Super Bowl MVP title.

During the 2016 season, Brady got swept into the Deflategate controversy and this led to Brady's suspension from the NFL for four games. Despite all that, Tom Brady did not buckle under the pressure and once again made a marvelous comeback by registering 11 wins out of the 12 games in the upcoming regular season, and two more wins were added to his name in the following postseason games. Brady's career in football was reaching new heights of success as he did not break his stride and continued to win title after title. The seventh time Brady returned to the Super Bowl, the Patriots claimed their fifth Super Bowl victory and Brady won the Super Bowl MVP title for a fourth time. Another record was associated with this win against the Atlanta Falcons, which was the record for the biggest comeback ever made in the history of the Super Bowl. This comeback refers to the Patriots recovery from being down by 25 points in the third quarter, and coming back to somehow win the game.

It was too with Brady as a starting quarterback that the Patriots were able to make an NFL record for lining up the most number of back-to-back victories (including playoffs). In the seasons of 2003 and 2004, the patriots secured 21 consecutive wins while also managing to break the record of maximum number of continuous victories with 10 playoff wins. The team also remained victors for the entirety of the 2007 season when the number of games per season had been increased to 16. Tom Brady stands first among the quarterbacks in the NFL postseason history in the context of throwing the highest number of touchdown passes for maximum yards. Brady has registered more than 1500 passing attempts in his quarterback career and established a career passing rating of 96.6 which puts him in the sixth highest position of all time.

After Joe Montana, Tom Brady is the only quarterback to have won as many NFL and Super Bowl MVP titles all of NFL history. Brady was chosen as the most valuable player again in 2007 while the press presented him with the honorable title of Male Athlete of the Year - the only other NFL player to hold this title had been Joe Montana. A remarkable number of records have been set in the history of NFL during Tom Brady's football career. Some of these records, in brief, are as follows: 50 touchdowns in a single season by Tom Brady the starting quarterback, the title of NFL MVP (Unanimous choice) earned by Tom Brady, Top ranking in NFL Top 100 league players, 358 uninterrupted passes, and the third best Touchdown to Interception ratio of 9:1. Also, the pairing of Tom Brady and Bill Belichick has been one of the best quarterback-coach pairings in the history of NFL with a total of 183 victories in regular season games and 25 post-season games.

Chapter Three: NFL Career

Season 2000

Tom was drafted with the 199th overall pick in the sixth round of 2000 NFL draft. This came as a shock to Brady and his family as they had hoped that a footballer of Brady's caliber would be drafted in the earlier rounds. However, the draft was a public event on TV and both Brady and his family were disheartened to find that six quarterbacks had already been drafted. This put terrible emotional strain on Tom Brady and he fled his home in embarrassment. When Brady finally got the notification of his drafting from the Patriots, Brady's reaction was priceless as he expressed his relief that he would not have to be an insurance salesman.

Brady was the final pick of the Patriots, which definitely worked in their favor considering Brady's magnificent list of honors. Initially, Brady was fourth on the depth chart, topped by two backup quarterbacks namely John Friesz and Michael Bishop and the starting quarterback Drew Bledsoe. As the season drew to a close, Tom had jumped two places up and was right behind Drew on the depth chart.

2001 season

For the first two games of the season 2001, Drew Bledsoe continued his starting job as a quarterback. The first match did not go in the favor of The Patriots and they faced a terrible loss with a six-point deficit, the final score calculating up to 23-17.

The second game of the 2001 season took place on the 23rd of September in which The Patriots went against New York Jets. In this game, the starting quarterback Bledsoe was injured during the fourth quarter when he took a hit from the linebacker of the New York Jets, Mo Lewis. As the second in line on the depth chart, the position of the starting quarterback was filled by Tom Brady in the final series of the match. The patriots lost the match to The New York Jets. In the third game of the season, The Patriots went up against the Indianapolis Colts and Brady held onto the starting job from the beginning of the game. The Patriots won the game with a score of 44 to 13 and Brady managed a passer rating of 79.6, which dropped to 58.7 in the following match against the Miami Dolphins, which led to The Patriots' loss.

The Patriots squared off against the San Diego Chargers in the fifth game of the season. Brady had eventually found his footing and showed improved performance with two scoring drives in the fourth quarter. The Patriots won with Brady managing to complete 33 passes out of the 54 attempts for 364 yards and two touchdowns. Brady's passer rating turned up to 148.3 in the following match at Indianapolis in the next week. The patriots scored 38 against 17 and stood victors. Led by Tom Brady as the starting quarterback, the Patriots secured 11 wins under their belt out of the 14 games they played. Brady's spectacular performance led the Patriots to win the AFC East and getting into the 2001-2002 playoffs. Brady registered a total of 18 touchdowns and around 2,843 passing yards.

2001 postseason

In the first game of the playoffs against the Oakland Raiders, the Raiders had a lead of 10 points against the Patriots. It was by the virtue of Brady's 312 yards thrown that the Patriots were able to make a comeback in the fourth quarter and finally take the lead. The game wasn't an easy win as a controversy had surrounded that game. Following a hit by Charles Woodson, the cornerback of the Oakland Raiders, Brady lost the possession of the ball. The ball was recovered by the Oakland Raiders, however, the "tuck rule" states that when a player is holding the ball for a forward pass, even a tentative movement of their arm begins a pass despite the player losing possession of the ball while tucking the ball back towards their body. If the ball has been successfully tucked back into the body and lost afterward, it becomes a fumble. By this rule, the referee announced it an incomplete pass.

Brady suffered a knee injury while playing against the Pittsburgh Steelers in the AFC championship and had to be backed up by Drew Bledsoe to defeat the Steelers. He recovered from his injury in time for the Super Bowl XXXVI, which was just held the following week in New Orleans and played against St. Louis Rams. The Patriots did not buckle under the powerful offense of the Rams and remarkably held their own all the way through three-quarters. With 90 seconds spared to regulation, the Rams were looking to tie the game and it seemed the Patriots were going to have to make the winning goal in overtime; this thought was shared by Coach John Madden. Rather with only seven seconds to spare, Brady chased the ball to Rams 31-yard line and spiked it to Adam Vinatieri who made the final goal (48-yard field goal) giving the Patriots a 3-point lead and winning them their first league championship. Brady was the first player to win a Super Bowl at such a young age and was titled the most valuable player in the league. Brady's starting job as the quarterback of the Patriots was secured with Drew's transfer to the Buffalo Bills.

2002 season

The Patriots failed to make it to the playoffs following a tie-up with the New York Jets and Miami Dolphins for the best record in the division. The third tiebreaker went in the favor of the New York Jets, winning them the division. And even if the Patriots would have made it to the playoffs, it was likely that they would not be able to hold their own in the very first round since Brady had suffered a shoulder injury and was trudging on with it for the majority of the second half of the season.

2003 season

The 2003 season paved the road for the Patriots' success in NFL. This was the season in which the Patriots bagged 12 back-to-back wins and ended the regular season with an AFC East victory. The statistics show that Tom Brady had a marvelous performance in the game against the Buffalo Bills where he managed to flourish a spectacular 122.9 quarterback rating. The season ended with Brady registering 23 touchdowns and 3,620 passing yards to his name.

2003 Postseason

The Patriots emerged victors over the Tennessee Titans and the Indianapolis Colts in the respective games of the playoffs. The Patriots became second-time league champions on the first of February in 2004 in the Super Bowl XXXVIII by defeating the Carolina Panthers with a score of 32 to 29 under the starting job of Tom Brady. Brady was once again given the honorable title of the Most Valuable player for a second time.

Brady managed to pull off throwing 354 yards and three touchdowns, also setting records as the quarterback with the most completions in a Super Bowl. The game would have been a tie if Brady hadn't pushed for a winning field goal with only 1:08 left on the clock.

2004 season

It was in this season when Brady led the Patriots to 21 continuous victories preceding the previous year and created a new NFL record. The Patriots finished the season with 14 wins and 2 losses, another record to signify their best ever performance as a defending champion. This year marked The Patriots' third AFC East victory in four years. Brady's game statistics by the end of the season were as follows: 3,692 passing yards, 28 touchdowns, and a passer rating of 92.6.

2004 postseason

Under the leadership of Tom Brady, the Patriots managed to defeat the Indianapolis Colts and the Pittsburgh Steelers in the AFC playoffs. Although Brady was running a high fever the night prior to the match against the Pittsburgh Steelers, Brady still managed to hold strong in the game and performed tremendously. His passer rating of 130.5 in this season topped all of his previous ratings. The Patriots once again won the championship for the third time in the Super Bowl XXXIX on the 6th of February 2005 after beating the Philadelphia Eagles 24 to 21.

2005 season

In the season of 2005, the burden of leading the Patriots to victory fell on the shoulders of Tom Brady when the running backs Corey Dillon, Patrick Pass, and Kevin Faulk fell victims to injuries. The positions were filled by Heath Evans as the running back and Russ Hochstein as the center, and Tom Brady had to get used to them to be able to work with them in proper coordination. This season marked 26 touchdowns for Brady to land him in the third position overall, and 4,110 passing yards putting him first in that category. His passer rating of 92.3 in this season was the second best of his career by that time. The Patriots marked the end of the season with a 10-6 record, and claimed another AFC East victory.

2005 postseason

The Patriots competed against Jacksonville Jaguars in the wild card round of the playoffs and defeated them with a score of 28 to 3. In this season, Brady lost for the first time in a playoff against the Denver Broncos who beat them with by 14-points on the fourteenth of January in 2006. Brady's performance statistics for the postseason included throwing for 341 yards, one touchdown, and two interceptions. The reason for Brady's below average performance in this season was later uncovered. The linebacker of The Patriots, Willie McGinest, revealed that Brady had a case of sports hernia and played the season regardless.

2006 season

The playoffs went in the favor of the Patriots, as they were able to pull off an 8 points lead and ended the game with a 12-4 record. The regular season ended with 24 touchdowns and 3,529 yards of throwing in Brady's account. Brady had been voted to the Pro Bowl two times prior to this season; however, during this season the offer made to him was to replace Phillip Rivers in the Pro Bowl when he suffered an injury. Brady turned the offer down.

2006 postseason

The wild card round went in The Patriots' favor as they managed to beat the New York Jets with 37-16. Brady threw for 212 yards and two touchdowns for 22-34. The divisional round against the Chargers in San Diego was Brady's first time playing a playoff game in his home state of California. The game did not seem to be going well for the Patriots as the chargers had an 8-points lead against them. However, the tables turned with Brady's pass to Reche Caldwell for 49 yards, which Stephen Gostkowski turned into a field-winning goal and ended the game with a 24-21 victory in the favor of the Patriots. The Patriots squared off against the Indianapolis colts for the title of the AFC championship. They had played against each other at Foxborough twice before, although the venue of this match was Indianapolis. The Patriots seemed to be winning when the game came to halftime with the Patriots leading with a score of 21-6, however, the game was flipped all the way in the second half when the Colts retaliated strongly and finished the game by beating the Patriots with a final score of 34-38.

2007 season

The 2007 season was an incredible one for Tom Brady. He set a new NFL record of 50 touchdown passes thrown. The Patriots also set the record for the NFL's first ever 16-win season.

Tom Brady was once again given the award of league MVP.

2007 postseason

In the first game of the postseason against the Jackson Jaguars, Brady set another NFL record for completion percentage in a game, with 92.9% on 26 of 28 completions, resulting in 3 touchdowns.

The Patriots went on to feature in the 2007 Superbowl against the Giants. In a low scoring affair, the Giants were victorious with a final score of 17 – 14. This marked the first time in history that an NFL team had remained undefeated all season, but not won the Superbowl.

2008 season

In 2008 the Patriots finished the regular season with a record of 11-5. Despite the good winning percentage, they did not qualify for the playoffs.

Tom Brady was injured in the very first game of the season, against the Chiefs. Tearing his anterior crucial ligament, Brady did not return for the remainder of the season.

2009 season

In the 2009 season, the Patriots finished with a 10-6 record, which was slightly worse than the previous year. Despite winning fewer games, this year the Patriots managed to qualify for the playoffs.

In Brady's return to the NFL against the Buffalo Bills, the Patriots managed a comeback victory by scoring 2 touchdowns in the final quarter, to overcome an 11-point deficit. In his first game for a year, Brady managed to register 378 yards thrown, and 2 touchdowns.

Later in the season, Brady set another NFL record for the most touchdowns in a single quarter, throwing 5 in the second term.

Brady would finish the season with 4,398 yards passing, and 28 touchdowns for a 96.2 rating. He suffered a broken finger and 3 fractured ribs during the season, but was able to overcome the injuries to be named the NFL's comeback player of the year.

The Patriots ended the regular season with a record of 10-6, qualifying them for the playoffs.

2009 postseason

The Patriots met the Ravens in the first game of the playoffs, and quickly fell behind. Tom Brady had a poor showing, and his three turnovers in the first quarter resulted in a 17-point lead for the Ravens.

The lead grew to a score of 24-0 which was simply too large for the Patriots to overcome.

The game and the season ended for the Patriots with a final score of 33-14. It was the Patriots first playoff loss at home in over 30 years.

2010 season

The Patriots registered a league-best record of 14-2 in the 2010 regular season. Tom Brady had another record-setting season, registering an NFL record 335 consecutive pass attempts without an interception. He also broke his own TD to INT ratio record with 9:1, and was once again named the league's MVP.

2010 postseason

The Patriots met the New York Jets in the first game of the postseason. Early in the game, Brady threw his first interception since week 5 of the regular season.

In a close battle, the Jets were victorious with a final score of 28-21. Despite their great performance in the regular season, the Patriot's season ended there.

2011 season

In the first week of the 2011 season, Brady performed exceptionally well in a game, contributing 4 touchdowns for his team. He even threw for 517 yards and aided one interception. The opponents, the Miami Dolphins were stunned as this was only the second time when he had gone for over 400 yards twice in a game.

In the results season finale against the Buffalo Bills, he became the fourth quarterback to throw for 5000 yards in a season. He ended the season with 5235 yards, surpassing Dan Marino's record of 5084. The Patriots finished the season with a record of 13-3 and grabbed the AFC's top seed.

2011 postseason

"There's no quarterback I'd rather have than Tom Brady. He's the best. He does so much for us in so many ways on so many different levels. I'm very fortunate that he's our quarterback and what he's able to do for this team. It's good to win with him and all the rest of our players. If that's more than somebody else did, I don't really care about that." –Bill Belichick

Brady accomplished his personal postseason best during the game against Denver Broncos, where the Broncos were defeated 45-10 by the Patriots. He tied with Daryle Lamonica and Steve Young for the record of throwing 6 touchdown passes.

This win was the first postseason win for the Patriots since the 2008 postseason, resulting in giving Brady and coach Belichick the record for maximum postseason wins by a quarterback-coach combo. They had 15 wins together. In the AFC championship game against the Baltimore Ravens, Brady did not throw a single touchdown pass although he did pass for 239 yards and scored a 1-yard rushing touchdown in the later stages of the game. The Patriots benefitted by a missed field goal by Ravens kicker Billy Cundiff and this enabled the Patriots to reach the Super Bowl for the fifth time with Brady's involvement.

In Super Bowl XLVI, the New York Giants faced off against the New England Patriots for the second time in five years. Brady played immensely well, and scored a record 96-yard touchdown to end the first half. At one point he completed 16 passes in a row. This was another Super Bowl record. He scored two touchdowns and one interception in the game and was penalized for grounding intentionally in the end zone. This allowed the Giants to win the game by a score of 21-17. Thus Brady was denied his fourth Super Bowl win.

2012 season

Brady starred in all 16 regular season games of the 2012 NFL season and led the Patriots to a 12–4 record. The Patriots scored 557 total points, the third highest in league history and Brady became the first quarterback to lead his team to 10 division titles. This also enabled him to end the year with 4827 yards. He further extended his touchdown streak and it was his third straight season where he scored 30 touchdowns.

2012 postseason

He played for the Patriots in both the games and crossed Joe Montana's record for most playoff wins in a career, winning his 17th game. Eventually, the Patriots lost to the Baltimore Ravens, who subsequently became the Super Bowl champions that year. Brady and the Patriots consented to a contract on Feb. 23, 2013, which extended Brady's services for three years and would keep him with the team through 2017. According to Peter King, it was an "amazing" deal because Brady collected only $27 million in the 2015, 2016 and 2017 seasons in new money. This contract also ensured owner Robert Kraft's desire that Brady would retire as a Patriot.

2013 season

The New England Patriots faced tough times during the opening of the season, as injuries and controversies plagued the team. Aaron Hernandez was arrested and Rob Gronkowski was injured. Players like Wes Welker and Danny Woodhead left for the Denver Broncos and San Diego Chargers respectively and Brandon Lloyd was released. In order to cover for the five players, the Patriots signed rookies Danny Amendola, Kenbrell Thompkins, Aaron Dobson and Josh Boyce. Brady was unfazed and completed 52% of his passes and scored three touchdowns in the first two games.

2013 postseason

The Patriots ended the 2013 season with a record of 12-4 and earned a first-round bye in the AFC. Brady appeared in his

25th playoffs against the Indianapolis Colts, thus breaking the record for the most appearances in the playoffs by a quarterback. The record had initially belonged to Brett Favre. The Patriots were eliminated by the Denver Broncos the next week, thus eliminating them from the playoffs.

2014 season

Brady started the 2014 season with a humiliating loss of 33-20 against the Miami Dolphins. It was the first time since 2003 that Brady lost an opening day game. He did, however, contribute with a 241-yard throw and a touchdown.

Later in the season, New England did make a comeback against the Minnesota Vikings but Brady struggled for form and threw for 149 yards and 1 touchdown for the team's 30-7 win. He was further put under pressure against the Oakland Raiders and could only score one touchdown. The Patriots lost to the Kansas City Chiefs by a humbling 41-14 margin but bounced back, winning the next two games against Cincinnati Bengals and Buffalo Bills. The New York Jets were further defeated by the Patriots and Brady excelled with a 261-yard show and three touchdowns.

The Patriots continued their winning streak with a 51-23 win over the Chicago Bears where Brady threw for 354 yards and scored a season-high 5 touchdowns. He continued his rich vein of form against the Broncos and Indianapolis Colts with a 333 and 257 yard run respectively. Brady then won against the Detroit Lions 34-9, passing 349 yards and scoring 2 touchdowns. The Greenbay Packers finally ended the Patriots' winning streak but Brady threw for 245 yards, scoring 2 touchdowns. Thus Brady was unsuccessful in securing the eighth consecutive win for the Patriots. The Patriots were again trailing by 14-3 against the San Diego Chargers but Brady lifted the team up with a 317-passing yard run with 2 touchdowns. The Patriots ended up winning the game by a score of 23-14. Brady then secured a record twelfth AFC East Division title with a 287-yard run and two touchdowns. He struggled again in the final couple of games, throwing for a mere 182 yards against the Jets while scoring a touchdown, and 80 yards against the Bills in a losing cause in the final match of the season. Brady only played in the first half of the game and Julian Edelman, Rob Gronkowski, and three starting offensive linemen did not play for the entire duration of the match.

2014 post-season

Brady threw for three touchdowns in the divisional round game against the Ravens. Joe Montana's record for the maximum number of playoff touchdowns was broken by Brady. The Patriots were down 14-0 after the Ravens scored quickly but the Patriots bounced back and equaled the score in the second quarter to 14-14. After a tumultuous game, which saw each side grabbing the lead from the other, Brady finally clinched his 9th AFC Championship game.

He then went on to play in his sixth Super Bowl. In Super Bowl XLIX he tied John Elway for most appearances in a Super Bowl. He completed 37 out of 50 passes for 328 yards, scored four touchdowns and made 2 interceptions to win the Super Bowl for the Patriots. It was his fourth Super Bowl title as he tied with Joe Montana and Terry Bradshaw for the record of most Super Bowl victories by a starting quarterback. He won the Super Bowl MVP for a record third time and tied Montana's record for most Super Bowl MVP awards. He also set a Super Bowl record of 37 complete passes, which would again be broken by him in Super Bowl LI, a couple of years later.

The publication of a 243-page report by NFL on the 6th of May in 2015 describing the controversy of deflating footballs in the recent AFC season made the claim that although he was not directly involved in the act of tampering with the balls, the Patriots' quarterback Tom Brady had known about it. Following the report and the substantial proof perpetuating the accusation, Brady faced a suspension penalty of four games from the NFL on the 11th of May. Brady was allegedly guilty of being privy to the dishonest act of deflation and not cooperating with the investigation process, rather showing resistance to it. In a letter written to Brady by the Executive vice president of football operations, it was stated, "Your actions as set forth in the report clearly constitute conduct detrimental to the integrity of and public confidence in the game of professional football. With respect to your particular involvement, the report established that there is substantial and credible evidence to conclude you were at least generally aware of the actions of the Patriots' employees involved in the deflation of the footballs and that it was unlikely that their actions were done without your knowledge. Moreover, the report documents your failure to cooperate fully and candidly with the investigation, including by refusing to produce any relevant electronic evidence (emails, texts, etc.), despite being offered extraordinary safeguards by the investigators to protect unrelated personal information, and by providing testimony that the report concludes was not plausible and contradicted by other evidence." With the help of NFLPA (NFL Players association), on 14th of May Brady made an appeal to challenge the penalty given to him.

However, the suspension was reinstated as it was announced by the commissioner of NFL, Roger Goodell on the 28th of July. Not satisfied with the outcome, Brady made the decision to appeal it again in the federal court through NFLPA.

According to Roger Goodell, one of the major factors that led to the continued suspension of Brady for four games was the resistance he put up in the investigation by destroying his cell phone. Not happy with how the state of events turned out to be against his favor, Brady made a post on his Facebook page clearly stating his disapproval with the decision. The post read, "I am very disappointed by the NFL's decision to uphold the 4 game suspension against me. I did nothing wrong, and no one in the Patriots organization did either... I will not allow my unfair discipline to become a precedent for other NFL players without a fight."

The controversy received mixed reactions. While some sided with Brady on the issue, other big names openly justified Brady's suspension from the games. One of them was the writer of Bleacher Report who expressed his opinion on the matter saying the suspension was a firm penalty but it was right. According to some of the people who commented on this matter, a possible reason for such harsh sentence to Brady could be the reputation of The Patriots for not abiding with/pushing the rules.

However, the suspension was revoked by the judge of the United States District Court for the Southern District of New York, Mr. Richard M. Berman on the day of September 3 of 2015. Consequently, Brady was given the permission to play in the four games of NFL season he was suspended from. The judge spoke in Brady's favor, mentioning NFL's shortcomings to give proper notice to Brady about the charges filed against him and the possible suspension it could result in. Goodell also received reprimands at the hearing for his manipulation of the testimony provided by Tom Brady.

The results of the NFL Kickoff game announced the Patriots the winner of the game under the starting job of Tom Brady. The Patriots beat the Steelers 28-21. With this win, Tom Brady broke the record of ex-quarterback of Green Bay Packers, Brett Favre, by becoming the starting quarterback with most number of wins (161 to be exact) in the regular season, all the while being on the same team. Brady performed just as remarkably in the second week as he did in the first. While Brady threw for 288 yards and four touchdowns in the first game, he threw in the second game for 466 yards and three touchdowns. Summing up the total of the initial five games of the season, Brady had added 14 touchdowns, one interception and a 118.4 quarterback rating into his account.

It seemed that the Patriots had started on the way downhill from there, the players on offensive positions were injured numerous times, Julian Edelman being one of them. With a 10-0 start, this state of events led the Patriots to face a terrible loss against Denver, even though they themselves were playing without their quarterback Peyton Manning. The Patriots went on to end the season with a record of 12-4. This put them with Denver Broncos and Cincinnati Bengals for the best record in AFC. Although the No. 1 seed in AFC went in Denver's favor as they had been victorious against the Patriots as well as the Bengals, The Patriots still managed the No.2 seed over the Bengals as they had performed better against their mutual opponents. Brady's solo record for the matter was the best of the season as he managed to pass for 36 touchdowns and seven interceptions. Brady was voted to his 11th Pro Bowl, which was also his seventh in a row. On the ranking list of the NFL Top 100 Players of 2016, Brady was put in the second position while the first position was claimed the most valuable player in the league, Cam Newton.

By this season, Julian Edelman had fully recovered from the foot injury he suffered in the previous season. United in all their glory, The Patriots managed a tremendous victory against the Chiefs, beating them to 27-20 in the divisional round. The title game of AFC took place at Mile High Stadium where The Patriots went against the Denver Broncos. Tom Brady played against Peyton Manning a total of 17 times in his career, this game being the last of their time together as Manning retired after this season. With only 17 seconds left in regulation, both the teams were tied up at a score of 18-18, however, when the Patriots' attempt at heading for a field goal failed, they went down by 2-points and lost the game 20-18. Brady had been able to complete only 27 passes out of 56, registered one touchdown, and intercepted twice.

2016 regular season

Tom Brady returned from his suspension of four games on October 9 straight into the 2016 season game between the Patriots and the Cleveland Browns. Brady performed marvelously with 28 completed passes out of the total attempted 40 for 406 yards and 3 touchdowns. The Patriots led the game with a 20 points margin. Brady's performance stayed just as fantastic in his game against Cincinnati Bengals, Brady leading the Patriots to a 35-17 victory. Brady passed for 376 yards and 3 touchdowns, managing to complete 29 passes out of 35. The Patriots' victory streak continued on as they beat the Pittsburgh Steelers by a score of 27-16 and the Buffalo Bills 41-25. Against the Steelers, Brady passed for 222 yards and two touchdowns, attempting 26 passes and completing 19 of them, while against the Bills registered 315 yards of passing for four touchdowns, and 22 completed passes out of 33. Brady's offensive nature in the games after his return from his suspension was so astounding that he was named the offensive player of the month.

In week 10, the Patriots went against the Seattle Seahawks. Both of the teams went all in and the game became tense as the lead switched 7 times, however, the Patriots ended up losing by a 7-point margin. The final score of the game was 31-24. Brady passed for 316 yards with no touchdowns and one interception, managing to complete 23 passes out of the total 32. Brady's next game was against the San Francisco 49ers, which was Brady's favorite team as a child. The Patriots won the game, beating the San Francisco 49ers to 30-17. Passing for 280 yards, no interceptions and four touchdowns, Brady completed 24 passes out 40.

Chapter Four: Personal Life and Political Views

Tom Brady had been in a relationship with Bridget Moynahan who is an actress from the year 2004 to 2006. Bridget revealed to the People Magazine that she was pregnant with Brady's baby on 18th of February 2007. Their relationship ended in late December of 2006, which was roughly around the same time Bridget got pregnant. Their son came into the world on 22nd August 2007 at Saint John's health center in Santa Monica, California.

Even though Tom Brady was there at the health center, he was not with Moynahan at the time of delivery. The boy was named Jon Edward Thomas Moynahan after Bridget's father Edward and Tom himself. After breaking it off with Moynahan, Brady got together with Brazilian Supermodel Gisele Bündchen in December of 2006. Brady spoke publicly about the events that led to them meeting, revealing they met on a blind date set up by a friend of theirs. Brady later got married to Gisele on the 26th of February, 2009.

The small Catholic marriage ceremony took place in Santa Monica, California. Gisele gave birth to her and Brady's son in 2009. Their second child together is a girl born in the year of 2012.

Brady has become so popular that he even got featured in some well-known television programs. Brady voiced his own character in an episode called Homer and Ned's Hail Mary Pass of The Simpsons, and another episode called Patriot Games of the popular TV series Family Guy. Tom Brady got a cameo role in a 2009 episode of the TV show Entourage where he acted as his own self, while in some other appearances in the movies

Entourage and Ted 2; Brady played tampered versions of himself. Tom Brady's elder sister Julie got married to Kevin Youkilis who is a baseball player, making Tom his brother-in-law.

With Brady's growing popularity and fame, he was asked to endorse some well-known brands such as Movado, Under Armour, Uggs and Glaceau Smartwater. Tom modeled for Stetson Cologne in 2007 and made an appearance in a commercial for the promotion of Simmons Bedding Company. Forbes magazine revealed that the year of 2014, Brady made $7-million from endorsements alone.

In the lieu of the recent presidential elections in America in 2016, Brady was found to be supporting the republican candidate Donald Trump who later became the President. Brady claimed that he had been friends with Donald Trump for 16 years and Donald Trump himself made a mention of Tom Brady while regarding a certain text message, which read that Brady was in full support of Donald Trump, and had voted in his favor. Controversially, Brady's wife's take on this matter was different as she answered in denial when questions started circulating about the couple's support for Trump on Instagram. Following the circulation of a photograph of a "Make America Great Again" cap in Tom's locker, Brady was again asked about his take on that year's political matters. However, Brady refused to give a clear answer saying that his wife had made a decision for them to not discuss politics and he was abiding by her decision. There had been some rumors about Tom Brady looking to pursue a political career in the near future and running for the position of a senator in the elections of 2018, but no such rumors have been confirmed yet.

Chapter Five: Most Notable Moments In His Career

With a career that spans 17 years and after playing 263 games, out of which he won 201, Tom Brady has had an impressive run!

Here is a list of 12 career defining moments from Tom Brady's life that have made him the man he is today!

Sept. 23, 2001: The Big Break

Brady was the Patriots' backup quarterback behind Drew Bledsoe and had only thrown about three passes in the pros up until that point. Late in the match between the Patriots and the Jets, Bledsoe was injured in a violent shoulder to shoulder hit by Mo Lewis, the linebacker of the Jets. This happened during the teams' Week 2 meeting.

So, after trying hard and failing to return to the game, Bledsoe was declared retired hurt and Brady, who was an extremely inexperienced quarterback then, was sent in. This was during the last few minutes of the game, and the Patriots lost 10 - 3.

As the season progressed, it was realized that Bledsoe's injury was a lot more severe than believed, and Brady had a more permanent spot in the team and aided the Patriots to have a record of 11-3 for the season. With his exceptional performance and a bit of tough luck on Bledsoe's end, Brady made his place in the team, emerging as one of the most iconic New England players.

Feb. 3, 2002: A Legend Is Born

It was the year after the deadly 9/11 attacks. The mood was somber and emotionally charged and Brady led the underdogs of the tournament. The Patriots were trailing by 14 points against the St. Louis Rams' Greatest Show on Turf. Marshall Faulk had proved to be the Offensive Player of the Year and their quarterback, Kurt Warner, was regularly the Most Valuable Player of the tournament. All the odds were against them.

The Rams drew the first blood when they scored the first quarter field goal, but the Patriots quickly hit back and scored during the three turnover opportunities they were providing, leading 17-3 during the third quarter of the game. The Rams ultimately scored and with 1:21 left on the clock, the teams were tied.

The Patriots had no timeouts remaining at their 21-yard line and conventionally it would have been more viable to take a knee and try to win the game during overtime. But, Brady proved that he was a mastermind by pushing the Patriots downfield and Adam Vinatieri was set up for the 48-yard Super Bowl winning goal.

The Patriots finished 27 - 16 and Brady was named MVP for 145 passing yards and scoring a touchdown. And that was the day when a legend was born.

Jan. 19, 2002: When The Rulebooks Came Out

Brady's first playoff game was nothing short of a drama. It was a Raiders vs. Patriots AFC divisional showdown. The home field was covered in a layer of snow. With 1:50 left on the clock, the Patriots were trailing 13-10. The patriots were at the 42-yard line of the Raiders.

Brady had the ball and he stepped back to pass. He faked a pump and tucked the ball instead. As this was happening, the cornerback of the Raiders, Charles Woodson, knocked the ball out of his hand and was concurrently retrieved by Greg Biekert, the linebacker. It was assumed that the season was over for the New England Patriots.

It was assumed by all that it was a fumble, but after further reviewing the footage from the game, Walt Coleman, the referee, announced that the call was being reversed according to the Rule 3, Section 21, Article 2 of the NFL rulebook as Brady's arm was moving forward. The rule read "any intentional forward movement of [the throwers] arm starts a forward pass, even if the player loses possession of the ball as he is attempting to tuck it back toward his body."

Adam Vinatieri scored a 43-yard field goal and tied the game and during overtime, he kicked yet another goal, winning the game for the New England Patriots. This was the last ever game to be played at the Foxboro stadium and was termed by Robert Kraft to be the best!

Sept. 30, 2001: The Beginning Of A Rivalry

This game was Tom Brady's first NFL start and the Patriots faced the Colts in this game. This game also saw the appearance of the young quarterback Peyton Manning. Though the Patriots blew the Colts out of the water, winning 44-13, and Brady's passer rating was 79.2 as opposed to Manning's 48.2, this was the beginning of the "greatest quarterback rivalry" in the history of the NFL.

Brady and Manning were never in the same division but went on to play 17 games against each other. Brady won that private tournament by winning 11 out of the 17 games, while Manning won only 6.

While the rivalry between the two players was legendary, the players had immense respect for each other and on his retirement, Manning mentioned that his handshake with Brady was one of the aspects of the NFL he would miss the most.

Feb. 1, 2004, and Feb. 6, 2005: Growing Bigger With Some Apprehensions

This was the time when Brady solidified his status as a future member of the NFL Hall of Fame after he led the New England Patriots to consecutive Super Bowl victories.

During the Super Bowl XXXVIII the Patriots began on a high and by the end of the third quarter, the patriots were leading 21 – 10. But, in the fourth quarter, Carolina crept into the game and took a 22-21 lead. With only 1:08 remaining on the clock, Brady led his team to victory by driving them down the field, leading to a classic Adam Vinatieri winning field goal. Brady received his second MVP after registering three touchdowns and throwing 354 yards.

The Brady-led Patriots won their third Super Bowl against the Eagles, after letting their opponents, Philadelphia, keep close. Philadelphia was leading with 1:48 on the clock and was in possession after the Patriots went for an onside kick and went three and out. But, luckily for the Patriots, Philadelphia wasn't able to cash in on their possession. Deion Branch, the Super Bowl MVP, was the star of the game with 133 yards and 11 catches, but it was Brady who continued to grow bigger.

But, with his growing success, there was a lot of speculation over his steep rise. A year later, a story was published when the Patriots' Spygate Scandal was broken, where ESPN wrote about the Eagles' accusation of cheating. According to the Eagles, the Patriots were a little too well prepared for their dime defense.

Apr. 16, 2005: The First Foray Into Entertainment

"He is a professional athlete, not a performer!" went through everybody's minds when it was announced that Brady would appear on Saturday Night Live.

This perspective changed after his appearance was aired, where he sang a long monologue describing his various talents that included, but were not limited to, speaking Japanese fluently, imitating Kermit the Frog and claims of killing a horse without any weapons.

Post his Saturday Night Live appearance, his acting career blossomed from there, from voicing in an episode of Family guy to small cameos on Entourage. But one of his most unexpected roles was that of a sperm donor in Ted 2.

His electric persona and good looks also landed him various prestigious and prominent product endorsements deals, one of the most well known being Uggs for men.

Sept. 7, 2008: An Injury That Led To A Big Loss

In the very first game of the 2008 season, the reigning MVP was hit real hard by Chiefs S Bernard Pollard on his left knee. Pollard was on the ground when he tried to sack off Brady. While on the ground, Pollard lunged for Brady's legs, accidentally hitting Brady's left knee with his helmet.

Brady walked off the field, but medical tests later revealed he had a torn Anterior Cruciate Ligament and Medial Collateral Ligament. This effectively ended his season in the opening game.

This news caused a lot of ripples through the league, as the Patriots were the favorites to win the Super Bowl the prior year, where they had a perfect regular season.

Matt Cassel, the backup quarterback, stepped into Brady's shoes for the rest of the season and led the Patriots to an 11-5 regular season record. Despite this record, the Patriots couldn't make it to the playoffs due to tiebreaker rules.

This incident also brought about a crucial change in the rules of the NFL: from the beginning of the 2009 season, no defensive player, who was already on the ground, was permitted to dive or lunge at the lower legs of a quarterback.

Jan. 2015–Oct. 2016: Deflategate? Who Cares?

When Brady led the New England Patriots to a massive victory over the Indianapolis Colts 45-7 during the AFC Championship game, it was the beginning of the Deflategate Era. The Colts had suspected that the Patriots were underfilling their balls, leading to a better grip and reduced fumbling. This led to a formal investigation, where the Patriots were found guilty and were fined $1-million. They also had to forfeit their first-round pick in the NFL 2016 draft and their fourth pick in the NFL 2017 draft.

Exactly 623 days later the Deflategate Era ended when the Patriots lost 16-0 to the Bills. During the course of those 623 days, Brady was handed a 4 game suspension, the suspension was revoked and the suspension was again enforced (while Brady played and won his fourth Super Bowl Ring.)

Over 623 days there was a lot of speculation that Brady would tarnish his legacy, but today, nobody really cares. Sure Brady "lost" to the NFL and had to serve his 4 game suspension, he still won in the end. Because despite all of the speculations, PSI level studies and broken cell phones – there is still no concrete evidence that Tom Brady was involved in this scandal.

Feb. 1, 2015: When A Scandal Breaks, Play On!

It is often said, "When people hate you, give them a reason".

Just as Deflategate broke and there were a lot of speculations of the Patriots cheating to win, the New England Patriots did not care. They had just one goal: Win the Super Bowl.

What did unfold was one of the most dramatic Super Bowls in the history of the tournament. The Patriots were playing against the Seahawks and were tied at 14-14 during the first half the game.

The offense of Brady and the Patriots was thwarted due to the talked about Seahawks defense. As the game was about to enter the final quarter, the Patriots went down 24-14.

The fans and the Patriots themselves seemed to have lost the hope of a win when Tom Brady decided that this was not how things were going to go down. When an almost perfect 68-yard touchdown drive reduced the Seahawks lead to just 3 from the earlier 7, Brady scored a perfect drive to catapult the Patriots into a 28 – 24 lead!

That year, Brady hoisted his fourth Super Bowl trophy, along with his third MVP trophy, cementing his image one of the greatest quarterbacks in the history of the NFL.

Conclusion

Once again, thank you for taking the time to read this book! I hope you found it to be informative, and that it was enjoyable to read about the NFL legend, Tom Brady.

If you enjoyed the book, please take the time to leave me a review on Amazon, it would be very appreciated!